7 Dinner Menus

TARLA DALAL
India's # 1 Cookery Author

S&C
SANJAY & CO.
MUMBAI

Second Printing : 2007

ISBN 10 : 81-89491-24-5
ISBN 13 : 978-8-189491-24-6

Price: Rs. 89/-

Published & Distributed by : **Sanjay & Company**
353/A-1, Shah & Nahar Industrial Estate, Dhanraj Mill Compound, Lower Parel (W), Mumbai - 400 013. INDIA.
Tel. : (91-22) 2496 8068 • Fax : (91-22) 2496 5876 • E-mail : sanjay@tarladalal.com

UK and USA customers can call us on :
UK : 02080029533 • USA : 213-634-1406
For books, Membership on **tarladalal.com**, Subscription for **Cooking & More** and Recipe queries
Timing : 9.30 a.m. to 7.00 p.m. (IST), from Monday to Saturday
Local call charges applicable

Recipe Research & Production Design
Arati Fedane
Umaima Abdually

Nutritionist
Nisha Katira
Sapna Thakkar

Food Stylist
Shubhangi Dhaimade

Photography
Jignesh Jhaveri

Typesetting
Adityas Enterprises

Design
Satyamangal Rege

Printed by :
Minal Sales Agencies, Mumbai

DISCLAIMER
While every precaution has been taken in the preparation of this book, the publishers and the author assume no responsibility for errors or omissions. Neither is any liability assumed for damages resulting from the use of information contained herein. And of course, no book is a substitute for a qualified medical advice. So it is wiser to modify your dietary patterns under the supervision of a doctor or a nutritionist.

BULK PURCHASES
Tarla Dalal Cookbooks are ideal gifts. If you are interested in buying more than 500 assorted copies of Tarla Dalal Cookbooks at special prices, please contact us at 91-22-2496 8068 or email : sanjay@tarladalal.com

INTRODUCTION

A homemaker's biggest dilemma is what to cook everyday. Even the most accomplished cooks and those who really enjoy their time in the kitchen find it difficult to dream up exciting menus for the family day after the day. Fussy children and complaining spouses don't help!

If you regularly dish up the same routine fare that both you and your family are thoroughly bored of, this book will help bring excitement into your cooking. We have put together 7 Dinner Menus from around the world, one for each day of the week, to help you transform into an instant gourmet chef! Treat your family to these imaginatively created Mexican, Thai, Chinese, American, Italian, Arabian and Indian menus, and watch their boredom turn to delighted surprise.

The menus consist of dishes typical to the various cuisines, though all the recipes have been modified from their authentic versions to appeal to the Indian palate. Easy to make, they require no difficult-to-obtain ingredients. In fact we have suggested easily available substitutes to ensure ease of preparation, such as *samosa patties* to make baklava and bread to make *koftas.* Each menu is a complete meal ranging from starter to dessert, and is guaranteed to please even fussy kids and tradition-bound elders.

Once you're confident about tackling the different menus, you could try your skills on a wider audience! Invite a few friends over and surprise them with a special theme party. Try out some of the decorating and entertaining tips we've added, and watch your reputation as a hostess soar!

Bon Appetit!

CONTENTS

MENU 1

Delhi ka Zaika

Phudina Lassi. 10
Hare Bhare Kebab 11
Quick Vegetable Korma 12
Kofta Biryani 14
Kale Angoor ka Raita 18
Seb ki Jalebi 20

MENU 2

Fiesta Mexicana

Nachos with Mango Salsa 24
Sweet Corn and Spring Onion Soup . . . 26
Bean and Vegetable Salad 27
Tortilla Bake 29
Fried Ice-cream with Butterscotch Sauce 33

MENU 3

Straight from Chinatown

Hot and Sour Soup 38
Vegetable Dumplings 39
Tofu Nests 42
Stewed Noodles 43
5 Spice Rice 45
Saiwoo Vegetables 47

MENU 4

Cucina Italiana

Bruchettas 52
Bean and Pasta Soup 54
Garden Fresh Salad 57
Basil and Tomato Pasta 59
Tiramisu 61

MENU 5

No Fuss American

Two in a Bowl Soup 67

Crunchy Salad 69

Pasta and Vegetable Casserole 71

Celery Garlic Toasts 73

Cream and Brownie in a Glass 74

MENU 6

Arabian Delights

Herbed Hummus with Sesame Lavash . 79

Labneh with Crispy Vegetables 81

Orange Sesame Tabouleh 83

Falafel 86

Baklava 89

MENU 7

Try Thai

Sweet Corn Cutlets 93

Som Tam (Green Soup Papaya Salad) . . 95

Phadthai (Thai Fried Noodles) 96

Red Curry 98

Green Rice 100

Temblaque 101

MENU 1

Delhi ka Zaika

About the Menu....

North Indian cuisine is a favourite across the country, its robust flavours appealing to the fussiest palate. Here we have a menu straight from the kitchens of Delhi, a combination of traditional recipes that have been subtly modified to introduce interesting new flavours.

Lassi gets a refreshing twist with phudina, its minty flavour whetting the appetite for more. Hare Bhare Kebabs make attractive starters, their colour complemented by the taste. Biryani gets an unusual new avatar, with bread koftas replacing regular vegetables. Quick Vegetable Korma instead provides you your daily dose of vegetables. Round off the menu with a sweet and sour raita using black grapes. For dessert, whip up apple jalebis, which are not only easier to make but also crunchier and healthier than the original.

If you are serving this menu at a party, make sure you evoke the atmosphere of Delhi with well-placed floral decorations using typical Indian flowers such as marigolds and strings of mogras. Create an eye-catching centrepiece with floating candles, diyas and a lotus or lily in bloom. Drape colourful scarves around the room and light up a few fragrant incense sticks to set the mood.

Phudina Lassi

Preparation time: 10 minutes.   Cooking time: Nil.   Serves 4.

1½ cups fresh curds *(dahi)*
½ cup chopped mint *(phudina)* leaves
½ tsp black salt *(sanchal)*
4 tbsp sugar
1 tsp cumin seed *(jeera)* powder
8 to 10 ice-cubes

For the garnish
A few mint (*phudina*) leaves

1. Combine all the ingredients except the ice, in a blender and blend for 2-3 minutes.
2. Add ½ cup of water and the ice-cubes and blend again for about 30 seconds.
   Serve immediately in small individual glasses garnished with mint leaves.

Handy tip : To make a salty version, just omit the sugar and add salt to taste instead.

Hare Bhare Kebab

Preparation time: 20 minutes. Cooking time: 20 minutes. Makes 8 kebabs.

1½ cups boiled and mashed potatoes
¼ cup finely chopped french beans
¼ cup finely chopped carrots
½ cup spinach (*palak*) leaves, torn into pieces
2 tbsp chopped coriander
2 tbsp chopped green chillies
1 tbsp chopped ginger
2 tsp fresh breadcrumbs
A few drops of green colour (optional)
A few drops of lemon juice
Salt to taste

Other ingredients
Oil for deep-frying

1. Mix all the ingredients except the oil and divide into 8 equal portions.
2. Shape each portion into a round and press the round lightly to make flat kebabs.
3. Deep-fry the kebabs in hot oil till they are golden brown.
4. Drain on absorbent paper.

   Serve hot.

Quick Vegetable Korma

Preparation time: 10 minutes. Cooking time: 20 minutes. Serves 4.

¼ cup cauliflower, cut into small florets
¼ cup chopped french beans
1 medium carrot, peeled and cubed
¼ cup green peas
1 medium capsicum, cubed
¼ cup baby corn, cut into slices
½ tsp cumin seeds *(jeera)*
2 medium onions, puréed, refer handy tip
2 cloves (*laung/lavang*)
1 stick cinnamon (*dalchini*)
1 cardamom (*elaichi*)
1 tsp ginger-garlic paste
½ tsp green chilli paste
1 cup milk
¼ cup *paneer* (cottage cheese), cut into small pieces
¼ cup pineapple slices (canned), cut the small pieces

3 tbsp cream
½ tsp *garam masala*
1 tbsp *ghee*
Salt to taste

For the garnish
1 pineapple slices (canned)
1 tbsp chopped coriander

1. Heat the ghee in a kadhai and add the cumin seeds. When the seeds crackle, add the onion purée, cloves, cinnamon, cardamom, ginger-garlic paste, green chilli paste and saute for 5 to 7 minutes while stirring continuously.
2. Add the cauliflower, french beans, carrot, green peas, capsicum, baby corn, salt, ½ cup of milk and ¼ cup of water. Cover and cook over a slow flame till the vegetables are tender.
3. Add the remaining milk, paneer, pineapple, cream and *garam masala* and cook for another 3 to 4 minutes.
   Serve hot garnished with pineapple slices and coriander.

Handy tip: To make purééd onions, just blend roughly chopped onions to a smooth paste in the blender.

Kofta Biryani

Preparation time: 30 minutes. Cooking time: 40 minutes. Serves 4.
Baking temperature : 200°C (400°F). Baking time : 20 to 25 minutes.

For the bread koftas
4 bread slices
2 tbsp finely chopped onions
2 green chillies, finely chopped
1 tbsp fresh curds *(dahi)*
A pinch soda bi-carb
1 tsp ginger-garlic paste
Salt to taste

For the rice
1 cup long grained rice
1 bayleaf (*tejpatta*)
1 stick cinnamon *(dalchini)*
2 cardamoms *(elaichi)*
2 cloves *(laung/lavang)*
Salt to taste

For the gravy
2 cloves (*laung/lavang*)
1 stick cinnamon *(dalchini)*
½ cup sliced onions
2 tsp ginger-garlic paste
1 tsp chilli powder
2 tsp coriander-cumin seed (*dhania-jeera*) powder
¼ tsp turmeric powder (*haldi*)
4 tomatoes, sliced
½ cup fresh curds (*dahi*)
¼ cup boiled green peas
3 tbsp oil
Salt to taste

Other ingredients
Oil for deep-frying

For the garnish
4 tbsp fresh curds (*dahi*)
2 tbsp chopped coriander
2 tbsp chopped mint (*phudina*) leaves

For the bread koftas

1. Combine all the ingredients except the oil with a little of water if required. Mash well.
2. Divide the mixture in 15 to 20 portions. Shape into even-sized rounds.
3. Deep-fry in hot oil till they are golden brown in colour.
4. Drain on absorbent paper. Keep aside.

For the rice

Cook the rice in 2 cups of hot water with the bayleaf, cinnamon, cardamoms, cloves and salt. Ensure that each grain of rice is separate. Keep aside.

For the gravy

1. Heat the oil in a pan and add the cloves and cinnamon.
2. Add the onions and sauté till they turn translucent.
3. Add the ginger-garlic paste, chilli powder, coriander-cumin seed powder and turmeric powder (*haldi*) sauté for 1 minute.
4. Add the tomatoes and salt and cook till the oil separates.
5. Add the curds and mix well, simmer for another 5 minutes.
6. Add the green peas and mix well. Keep aside.

How to proceed

1. Whisk the curds, coriander and mint with 4 tbsp of water. Keep aside.
2. Arrange the gravy at the bottom of a baking dish.
3. Top with the bread koftas and cover with the cooked rice.
4. Top with the curds mixture.
5. Cover with a lid and bake in a pre-heated oven at 200°C (400°F) for 15 to 20 minutes.
   Serve hot.

Handy tip : You could use a heavy bottom pan and cook on the gas on a very low flame if you do not want to use the oven.

Kale Angoor ka Raita

Preparation time: 10 minutes. Cooking time: Nil. Serves 4.

1 cup finely chopped black grapes
1 cup beaten fresh curds (*dahi*)
½ tsp black salt *(sanchal)*
1 tsp cumin seed *(jeera)* powder
½ tsp chilli powder
Salt to taste

1. Put the grapes in a bowl and mash them slightly.
2. Add the black salt, cumin seed powder, chilli powder and salt and mix well.
3. Keep aside for 10 to 15 minutes.
4. Add the curds, mix well and refrigerate.
   Serve chilled.

SEB KI JALEBI : Recipe on page 20. →

Seb ki Jalebi

Picture on page 19.

Preparation time: 15 minutes. Cooking time: 20 minutes. Makes 8 jalebis.

8 apple rings
¾ cup plain flour *(maida)*
¼ tsp dry yeast
1 tsp sugar
1 tbsp melted ghee

For the sugar syrup
1 cup sugar
½ tsp saffron *(kesar)*
2 tsp rose water

Other ingredients
Oil for deep-frying

For the garnish
½ tsp cardamom (*elaichi*) powder
1 tbsp blanched and sliced pistachios
A few rose petals

For the syrup

1. Dissolve the sugar in 1 cup of water and boil for 5 minutes. The syrup should be of 1 thread consistency.
2. Warm the saffron in a small vessel, add a little milk and rub until the saffron dissolves. Add this to the syrup.

3. Add the rose water. Keep aside.

How to proceed

1. Add the yeast and 2 pinches of sugar to ½ cup of lukewarm water. Mix well.
2. Sprinkle 2 pinches of flour on top. Cover and keep for 3 to 4 minutes. If the cup is full of froth, the yeast is ready to use.
3. Mix the flour, yeast liquid, sugar, melted ghee and some warm water and whisk until the mixture has the consistency of thick batter.
4. Cover and keep for 40 to 50 minutes. Mix well again.
5. Dip apple rings in this batter and deep-fry in oil on both sides until crisp. Drain on absorbent paper and keep aside.
6. Heat the syrup till warm, remove from the flame and drop apple rings into it.
7. Soak for 1 minute and drain.
8. Garnish with cardamom powder, pistachios and rose petals.
   Serve hot.

MENU 2

Fiesta Mexicana

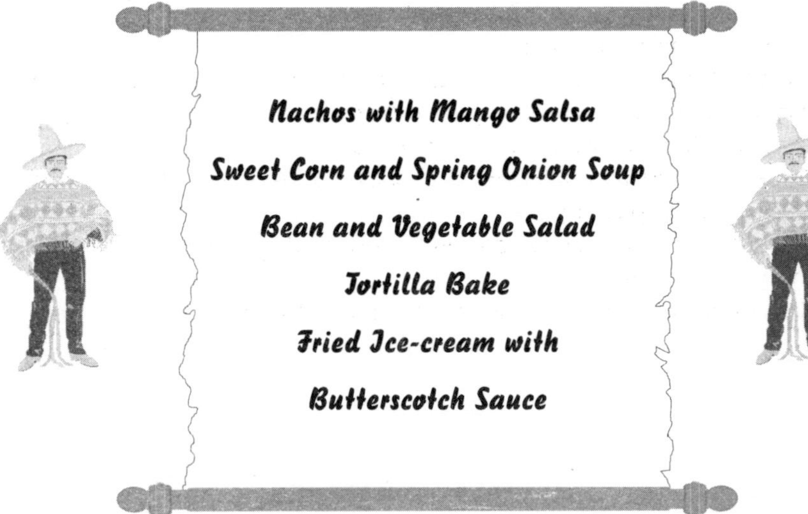

Nachos with Mango Salsa

Sweet Corn and Spring Onion Soup

Bean and Vegetable Salad

Tortilla Bake

Fried Ice-cream with
Butterscotch Sauce

About the Menu....

Mexican cooking is a lot like Indian cooking…full-bodied, colourful, infinitely textured and a delight to the senses! It uses ingredients that are easy to find and quick to prepare. Our Mexican menu includes a few authentic dishes that are not yet popular outside the country, in addition to several that are more easily recognisable.

Start off with Nachos, the popular corn chips found in every corner of Mexico. Serve them with an unusual mango salsa, a wonderfully tart dip that acquires a hidden sweetness with the addition of the tropical fruit, or citrus substitutes like oranges or sweet lime. Corn is a national staple in Mexico and combines well with spring onions to make a really delicious soup; while crunchy garlic flavoured croutons and a sharp mustard dressing add a zing to the Bean and Vegetable Salad. The Tortilla Bake, sumptuous layers of beans and vegetables smothered with white sauce, is a filling main course that deserves a stylish dessert! Though Fried Ice Cream is not an original Mexican dessert, it is served in most Mexican restaurants, and the trick lies in maintaining temperatures of both oil and ice cream.

When you plan a Mexican theme, think vibrant and vivacious. Pick one element you would like to emphasise and highlight it dramatically. Use clusters of brightly coloured capsicum (bell peppers), large bhavnagri chillies or small bird chillies to spice up your dinner table. For a really wild time, conduct a chilli eating competition! And keep the margaritas flowing.

Nachos with Mango Salsa

Preparation time: 10 minutes. Cooking time: 10 minutes. Serves 4.

1 cup finely ground maize flour (*makai ka atta*)
¾ cup plain flour (*maida*)
1½ tsp carom seeds (*ajwain*), optional
½ tsp cumin (*jeera*) seeds
1 tbsp oil
Salt to taste

Other ingredients
Oil for deep-frying

To be mixed together into a mango salsa (for serving)
½ cup chopped ripe mangoes
½ cup chopped tomatoes
1 tbsp chopped spring onion whites
1 tbsp chopped spring onion greens
½ tsp chopped green chilli

1 tbsp chopped coriander
A pinch of sugar
Salt to taste

1. Roast the cumin seeds on a *tava* (griddle) for a few seconds.
2. Add the carom seeds and roast again for a few seconds. Pound them coarsely.
3. Mix all the ingredients together and make a dough by adding warm water. Knead very well.
4. Divide the dough into small portions.
5. Roll out each portion into thin rotis with the help of a little flour, prick all over with a fork. Cook lightly on a *tava* (griddle).
6. Cut each roti into 25 mm x 25 mm. (1″ x 1″) squares and deep-fry in hot oil until crisp.
7. Drain thoroughly on absorbent paper. Store in an air-tight tin.
   Serve with the mango salsa.

Sweet Corn and Spring Onion Soup

Picture on page 1.

Preparation time: 5 minutes. Cooking time: 7 to 8 minutes. Serves 4.

2½ cups boiled sweet corn kernels (*makai ke dane*)
1 cup milk
¾ cup chopped spring onions
2 tbsp plain flour *(maida)*
2 tbsp butter
Salt to taste
Pepper to taste

1. Blend the corn, milk and spring onions into a smooth purée in a mixer. Keep aside.
2. Heat the butter in a saucepan and sauté the flour in it for ½ minute or till you get the aroma of cooked flour.
3. Add the corn mixture, 2 cups of water, salt and pepper and cook for 4 to 5 minutes. Serve hot.

Bean and Vegetable Salad

Preparation time: 20 minutes.   Cooking time: 20 minutes.   Serves 4.

½ cup *kabuli chana* (chick peas)
2 cups lettuce leaves, torn
1 cup peeled and cubed cucumber
½ cup capsicum cubes
2 tbsp chopped celery
1 cup tomato cubes
½ cup chopped spinach *(palak)*
Salt to taste

For the garlic croutons
4 bread slices
½ tsp grated garlic
1½ tbsp butter

To be mixed into a dressing
½ tsp grated lemon rind
2 tbsp olive oil or salad oil
Juice of 1 lemon
½ tsp mustard (*rai/sarson*) powder
1 tbsp chopped parsley
Salt to taste

For the garlic croutons

1. Cut the bread slices into 12.5 mm. (½″) cubes.

2. Heat the butter in a non-stick pan and add the garlic.
3. Add the bread cubes and sauté over a medium flame till they are lightly browned and crisp. Cool completely.

How to proeed

1. Wash and soak the *kabuli chana* overnight. Drain.
2. Pressure cook it with salt and 3 cups of water for 2 to 3 whistles until they are cooked. Drain out all the water and cool completely.
3. Combine all the other ingredients including the chick peas in a large bowl and refrigerate till use.
4. Just before serving, add the garlic croutons and the dressing and toss lightly. Serve immediately.

Tortilla Bake

Preparation time: 30 minutes. Cooking time: 30 minutes. Serves 4.
Baking temperature : 200°C (400°F). Baking time : 20 minutes.

For the tortillas

¾ cup maize flour *(makai ka atta)*
¾ cup plain flour *(maida)*
4 tsp oil
¾ tsp salt

For the refried beans

1 cup red kidney beans *(rajma)*, soaked overnight
½ cup sliced onions
1 clove garlic, chopped
3 green chillies, chopped
1 cup chopped tomatoes
2 tsp sugar
1 tsp roasted cumin seed *(jeera)* powder
2 tbsp butter
2 tbsp oil
Salt to taste

For the vegetable layer

½ cup sliced onion
¼ cup chopped capsicum
½ cup corn kernels (*makai ke dane*)
1 cup sliced mushrooms
1 tsp Tabasco sauce
1 tbsp oil
Salt and pepper to taste

For the white sauce

1 tbsp plain flour *(maida)*
1 cup milk
1 tbsp butter
Salt and pepper to taste

For the garnish

Grated cheese

For the tortillas

1. Knead both the flours, oil and salt with enough warm water to a soft dough.
2. Divide the dough into 3 equal parts and roll out each portion into chapati of 175 mm. (7″) diameter.

3. Cook each chapati lightly on a *tava* (griddle) and keep aside.

For the refried beans

1. Wash and soak the beans overnight. Next day, drain and keep aside.
2. Heat the butter and oil in a pan and sauté the onions in it till they turn translucent.
3. Add the garlic and green chillies and sauté for a few more minutes.
4. Add the tomatoes, sugar, cumin seed powder and salt.
5. Stir for a few minutes and add the beans and ½ cup of water.
6. Pressure cook till the beans are cooked (about 4 to 5 whistles).
7. When done, mash lightly and keep aside.

For the vegetable layer

1. Heat the oil in a pan and stir-fry the onions, capsicum, corn kernels and mushrooms in it till they are soft.
2. Add the Tabasco sauce, salt and pepper and mix well. Keep aside.

For the white sauce

1. Melt the butter in a pan, add the flour and sauté on a slow flame for ½ minute or till you get the aroma of cooked flour.
2. Add the milk gradually and stir continuously until the sauce thickens.
3. Add the salt and pepper and mix well. Keep aside.

How to proceed

1. Grease a 200 mm. (8") ovenproof dish with butter.
2. Place one tortilla on the bottom of this dish.
3. Spread the refried beans over the tortilla.
4. Place another tortilla on top.
5. Top with the vegetable layer, the third tortilla and the white sauce.
6. Garnish with grated cheese and bake in a pre-heated oven at 200°C (400°F) for 15 minutes.

   Serve hot.

Fried Ice-cream with Butterscotch Sauce

Picture on page 2.

Preparation time: 30 minutes. Cooking time: 5 minutes. Serves 4.

8 scoops of vanilla ice-cream
1 cup milk
Fresh bread crumbs to coat

Other ingredient
Oil for deep-frying

For the butterscotch sauce
½ cup sugar
1 tbsp butter
4 tbsp fresh cream
¼ tsp vanilla essence

For the butterscotch sauce

1. Heat the sugar in a non-stick pan and allow it to caramelize to a light brown colour.
2. Remove from the flame and add ¼ cup of hot water. Place on a slow flame and make a syrup of one string consistency.
3. Add the butter and cream and mix well.
4. Allow it to simmer for 5 to 7 minutes till the sauce is of a honey consistency.
5. Cool completely and keep aside.

How to proceed

1. Line a tray with butter paper. Adjust your fridge temperature to low.
2. Place the scoops on the tray at 25 mm (1″) distance and keep in the freezer till they harden.
3. Dip the hardened ice-cream balls in milk and roll in bread crumbs till coated properly.
4. Put them back in the freezer to harden.
5. Coat the ice-cream balls for about 3 to 4 times till a thick coating is achieved.
6. Heat oil on high flame in a *kadai*.
7. Remove ice cream balls from fridge (only 2 at a time) and dip in hot oil, make sure the balls are completely immersed in the oil. Don't turn them while frying, just dip and remove.
8. When balls turn golden colour remove and serve immediately with butterscotch sauce. Repeat for the remaining ice cream to make more balls.

Handy tips : 1. Crushed cornflakes / desiccated coconut also make great coatings.
2. Ensure that fried ice-cream is consumed immediately.

MENU 3

Straight from Chinatown

About the Menu....

Indians have taken to Chinese food with much enthusiasm, even creating a unique Indo-Chinese version of it that can be found at street corners across the country.

In this menu, we use all-time favourite Hot and Sour Soup and follow it up with crisp Vegetable Dumplings served with a range of piquant sauces. While the delicate Tofu Nests might look difficult to create, we've introduced a short cut in the form of readymade spring roll wrappers! Stewed Noodles are drenched in a delectable sauce and do not require an accompanying gravy. Rice lovers will be amazed at how different the 5 Spice Rice is from the usual fried rice. The sweet and spicy Saiwoo Vegetables can be served either with the main course or as a starter.

It's not difficult to create an Oriental mood. All you need is some pretty Chinese lanterns and fans artfully arranged around the room. Play some soft tinkling music in the background and make sure you have chopsticks at hand for a guest who wants to be really authentic.

SAIWOO VEGETABLES : Recipe on page 47. →

Hot and Sour Soup

Preparation time: 20 minutes. Cooking time: 5 minutes. Serves 4.

¼ cup shredded cabbage
¼ cup grated carrots
¼ cup finely chopped cauliflower
¼ cup chopped spring onions whites
2 pinches MSG (*Mono Sodium Glutamate*)
3 cups clear vegetable stock, page 44
1 tablespoon soya sauce
1 teaspoon chilli sauce
1 tablespoon chopped coriander
3 tablespoon cornflour dissolved
in ½ cup water
2 tablespoons oil
Salt and freshly ground pepper to taste

For the garnish
1 tbsp chopped spring onion greens

1. Heat the oil in a wok over a high flame. Add the cabbage, carrots, cauliflower, spring onions and MSG and stir fry over a high flame for 2 minutes.
2. Add the stock, soya sauce, chilli sauce, coriander, salt and pepper and simmer for 2 minutes.
3. Add the cornflour mixture and boil for 3 to 4 minutes while stirring continuously.
4. Mix in vinegars and switch off the flame.

Serve hot, garnished with spring onion greens.

Vegetable Dumplings

Preparation time: 15 minutes. Cooking time: 30 minutes. Makes 25 dumplings.

For the dough
1½ cups plain flour *(maida)*
2 tbsp oil
Salt to taste

For the vegetable filling
½ cup shredded cabbage
½ cup shredded carrot
¼ cup finely chopped mushrooms
¼ cup finely chopped asparagus
2 tsp finely chopped ginger
½ tsp pepper powder
2 tbsp soya sauce
Salt to taste

For the red sauce
1 tomato
3 cloves garlic
2 whole dry red chillies, broken into pieces
Salt to taste

For the black sauce
½ cup soya sauce
1 tbsp honey
2 tsp vinegar
2 tsp roasted sesame seeds *(til)*
Salt to taste

For the vegetable filling

1. Heat the oil in the wok, add the ginger and sauté for for a while.
2. Add all the remaining ingredients and sauté for a few more minutes.
3. Remove from heat and divide into 25 equal portions. Keep aside to cool.

For the red sauce

1. Boil a vesselful of water and put the tomato in it for a few minutes. Remove, peel and keep aside.

2. Dry roast the red chillies till they are crisp.
3. Combine the tomato, garlic, dry red chillies and salt and blend to a smooth sauce. Keep aside.

For the black sauce

Combine all the ingredients and mix well. Keep aside.

How to proceed

1. Combine all the ingredients together for the dough and knead into a soft pliable dough.
2. Roll out into a big cylinder.
3. Divide into 25 equal portions.
4. Roll out each portion into very thin circle of approx. 50 mm .(2") diameter.
5. Place one portion vegetable filling in the centre of the rolled circle.
6. Bring together the edges and pinch them with your fingertips to make dumplings.
7. Repeat with the remaining dough and filling to make 24 more dumplings.
8. Steam in a greased steamer for about 10 minutes.
   Serve hot with the red and black sauces.

Tofu Nests

Preparation time: 10 minutes. Cooking time: 5 minutes. Makes 8.

1 cup grated tofu (soya *paneer*)
2 tbsp Schezuan sauce
2 tbsp corn flour
10 spring roll wrappers
Salt to taste
Oil for deep-frying

1. Cut the spring roll wrappers into thin strips of approx 3 mm diameter. Keep aside.
2. Make a cornflour mixture by dissolving 1 tbsp of cornflour in 2 tbsp of water.
3. Combine the tofu, Schezuan sauce, 1 tbsp of corn flour and salt.
4. Divide into 8 equal portions and shape each portion into a ball.
5. Dip each ball in the cornflour mixture and then roll them in the spring roll wrapper strips.
6. Flatten a little and deep-fry in hot oil till golden brown.
7. Drain on absorbent paper and serve hot.

Stewed Noodles

Preparation time: 10 minutes. Cooking time: 15 minutes. Serves 4.

3 cups boiled noodles
½ cup Chinese green melon, cut into cubes
½ cup coloured capsicum (yellow, green, red), cut into cubes
¼ cup carrot strips, blanched
¼ cup dry shitake mushrooms (optional)
½ cup broccoli florets, blanched
4 nos. baby corn, sliced and blanched
2 cups clear vegetable stock
2 tbsp cornflour
2 tbsp soya sauce
Salt and pepper to taste

1. Soak the mushrooms in lukewarm water for about 15 minutes.
2. Drain and discard the water. Keep the mushrooms aside.
3. Heat the oil in a wok and sauté all the vegetables well on a high flame.
4. Dissolve the cornflour in the stock and add the mixture to the wok.

5. Stir in the soya sauce, salt and pepper.
6. Adjust the water consistency to make a thin sauce.
7. Cook all the vegetable in the sauce for 5 minutes.
8. Add the noodles and bring to a boil.
   Serve immediately.

Handy tip : To make vegetable stock, just add the vegetables like carrots, spring onions, capsicum and white pumpkin to a vesselful of water and simmer for about 20 minutes. Strain, use the liquid as stock and discard the vegetables.

5 Spice Rice

Preparation time: 15 minutes. Cooking time: 20 minutes. Serves 4.

3 cups Chinese rice, recipe below
1 cup fried tofu (soya *paneer*)
½ cup bean sprouts
1 cup sliced spring onions
1½ tsp Chinese 5 spice powder, see handy tip
A pinch sugar
2 tbsp oil
Salt to taste

For the Chinese rice
1 cup long grained rice
2 tbsp oil
1 tsp salt

For the Chinese rice

1. Wash the rice thoroughly and soak in 3 cups of water for 30 minutes. Drain and keep aside.

2. Boil 6 to 8 cups of water, add salt and 1 tbsp of oil.
3. Add the rice to the boiling water. Cook till the rice is 85% cooked.
4. Pour into a colander and let the water drain out. Pour some cold water on the rice to arrest further cooking.
5. Let all the water from the rice drain out ensuring that the rice does not contain any moisture.
6. Add the remaining 1 tbsp of oil and toss the rice in it.
7. Spread the cooked rice on a flat surface till it is cool.
   Use as required.

How to proceed

1. Heat the oil in a pan, add the spring onions and sauté till they are tender.
2. Add the Chinese 5 spice powder and sauté for ½ a minute.
3. Add the bean sprouts and tofu and mix well.
4. Add the rice, sugar and salt and toss well.
   Serve hot.

Handy tip : 5 Spice Powder is a powdered mixture of fennel seeds (*saunf*), cloves (*laung / lavang*), cinnamon (*dalchini*), star anise (*dagad phool*), schezuan peppers in the ratio 1 : ½ : 1 : 2 : 2. It is slightly sweet and pungent and has to be stored tightly covered, in a dry place at room temperature.

Saiwoo Vegetables

Picture on page 37.

Preparation time: 20 minutes. Cooking time: 15 minutes. Serves 4.

For crispy vegetables
2 cups vegetables (carrots, baby corn, capsicum, zucchini), cut into thick strips
5 tbsp cornflour
2 tbsp water

For the honey 5-spice sauce
2 tbsp honey
2 tsp soya sauce
A pinch MSG (Mono Sodium Glutamate) optional
2 tsp sugar
½ tsp Chinese 5 spice powder, page 46
Salt to taste

Other ingredients
½ cup spring onion whites, chopped
2 tsp garlic, chopped
2 tbsp ginger, chopped

2 green chillies, sliced
4 dry red chillies, broken
¼ cup spring onion greens, chopped
2 tbsp Schezuan sauce
2 tbsp oil
Salt to taste

Other ingredients
Oil for deep-frying

For the crispy vegetables
1. Make a paste with water and the cornflour and add to the vegetables.
2. Mix lightly so that the batter coats the vegetables.
3. Deep fry the vegetables in hot oil until crisp. Remove, drain on absorbent paper and keep aside.

For the honey 5-spice sauce
1. Heat the honey over a low flame.
2. Add the MSG, soya sauce, Chinese 5 spice powder, sugar and salt and mix well.

3. Mix well and keep aside.

How to proceed

1. Heat 2 tablespoons of oil and add the spring onion whites, ginger, garlic and sauté for a few seconds.
2. Add the dry red chillies and green chillies and sauté till the red chillies turn brown.
3. Add the Schezuan sauce, honey 5-spice sauce and salt and cook for a few seconds.
4. Toss in the crispy fried vegetables and spring onion greens and serve immediately.

Handy tip : Do not cook for a long time after adding the vegetables as the vegetables will get soggy.

MENU 4

Cucina Italiana

About the Menu....

Italy is a nation of simple and rustic food, lovingly prepared and well presented. Italians love to cook, and enjoy sharing food with friends and family, turning even the simplest meal into a celebration.

Our Italian menu is a mix of hearty, flavourful fare with a generous dose of fresh vegetables. The rich tomato-flavoured Bean and Pasta Soup is a heavy start but the rest of the meal is much lighter. Bruchettas are garlic flavoured bread slices that can accompany the soup or be nibbled upon throughout the meal. The Garden Fresh Salad is a mouth-watering combination of lettuce, tomatoes, chickpeas, spring onions and paneer tossed in an aromatic basil-garlic dressing, while the main course of Basil and Tomato Pasta is a traditional favourite. An eggless Tiramisu rounds off the meal in a burst of intense flavour!

An Italian meal requires a simple setting bright checked tablecloths, some colourful flowers, chunky candles and bottles of red wine. It's the food that really sets the mood here, but bring out the operatic music if you think your guests will appreciate it.

Bruschettas

Preparation time: 20 minutes. Cooking time: a few minutes. Serves 4.
Baking temperature : 150°C (300°F). Baking time : 5 to 7 minutes.

8 slices of French bread
¼ cup tomato cubes
½ cup red capsicum cubes
½ cup yellow capsicum cubes
¼ cup zucchini or cucumber cubes
¼ cup mozzarella cheese cubes
Salt to taste

To be ground into a pesto paste
½ cup basil leaves
2 tbsp pine nuts (*chilgoza*)
2 cloves garlic
6 tbsp olive oil
Salt to taste

1. Mix the tomatoes, red capsicum, yellow capsicum, zucchini, mozzarella cheese and salt in a bowl to make the topping mixture and keep aside.
2. Spread the pesto paste on the French bread slices and place the topping on the slices.
3. Grill in a pre-heated oven at 150°C (300°F) for 2 to 3 minutes.
   Serve hot.

Handy tip : You can adjust the quantity of oilve oil in the pesto to get a spreading consistency.

Bean and Pasta Soup

Preparation time: 10 minutes. Cooking time: 15 minutes. Serves 4.

½ cup canned baked beans
¼ cup sliced onions
½ tbsp sliced garlic
1 cup chopped tomatoes
¼ cup macaroni or any small pasta
2 tsp cornflour
1 tsp dried oregano
2 tbsp cream
2 tbsp tomato ketchup
2 tbsp butter
Salt and freshly ground pepper to taste

For the garnish
4 tbsp grated Parmesan cheese or processed cheese

BASIL AND TOMATO PASTA : Recipe on page 59. →

1. Heat the butter in a pan, add the onions and garlic and sauté till the onions turn translucent.
2. Add the baked beans, tomatoes, macaroni, salt and 4 cups of hot water and bring to a boil. Simmer till the macaroni is cooked (approx. 8 to 10 minutes).
3. Dissolve the corn flour in 2 tbsp of water and add to the soup.
4. Add the oregano, cream, tomato ketchup, salt and pepper and mix well.
   Serve hot garnished with cheese.

Garden Fresh Salad

Preparation time: 10 minutes. Cooking time: 5 minutes. Serves 4.

1 cup torn mixed lettuce (frisse, iceberg, lollo rosso etc.)
3 tomatoes
10 to 12 deseeded and sliced black olives
1 cup cooked *kabuli chana* (chick peas)
1 cup cooked penne pasta
1 cup chopped spring onions
½ cup *paneer* (cottage cheese) cubes

For the dressing
3 tbsp olive oil
½ tbsp sliced garlic
2 tbsp chopped basil leaves
1 tsp dry red chilli flakes
Salt to taste

For the dressing

1. Heat the oil in a pan, add the garlic and sauté till it is browned.
2. Strain the garlic out of the oil and discard. Add the chopped basil and salt to the olive oil and keep aside till it cools. Add the chilli flakes and mix well.

How to proceed

1. Marinate the paneer in the prepared dressing, mix well and keep aside for 10 to 15 minutes.
2. Put the tomatoes in a vesselful of boiling water for 2 minutes.
3. Peel, deseed, chop them finely put in a serving bowl.
4. Add the lettuce, olives, *kabuli chana*, pasta, spring onions and refrigerate till use.
5. Just before serving, add the paneer and the dressing to the salad and toss well. Serve immediately.

Basil and Tomato Pasta

Picture on page 55.

Preparation time: 15 minutes. Cooking time: 15 minutes. Serves 4.

3 cups cooked bow (farfalle) pasta

For the basil and tomato sauce
1½ cups tomato pulp, refer handy tip
½ cup finely chopped onions
1 tbsp chopped garlic
1 tsp chilli powder
2 tbsp tomato purée
1 tsp sugar
4 to 5 tbsp fresh cream
12 to 15 basil leaves, chopped
2 tbsp olive oil or butter

For the garnish
4 tbsp grated Parmesan cheese or processed cheese

For the basil and tomato sauce

1. Heat the olive oil in a pan, add the onions and garlic and sauté till the onions turn translucent.
2. Add the tomato pulp and cook till the sauce thickens (approx. 5 to 7 minutes).
3. Add the chilli powder, tomato purée, sugar, salt and ½ cup of water and bring to a boil.
4. Add the cream and basil leaves. Mix well and keep aside.

How to proceed

Just before serving, re-heat the basil and tomato sauce and toss the bow pasta in it. Serve hot garnished with cheese.

Handy tip : Tomato pulp is made by blanching whole tomatoes in hot water and thereafter peeling, deseeding and chopping them.

Tiramisu

Preparation time: 20 minutes. Cooking time: a few minutes. Serves 4 to 6.
Setting time : 4 to 6 hours. Baking temperature : 160°C (320°F).
Baking time : 25 minutes.

1 ready-made 200 mm. (8") vanilla sponge cake
1 recipe cream cheese, given below
½ cup sugar
¼ cup Marsala or Port wine
1 cup chilled fresh cream

To mixed into a coffee soaking syrup
1 tsp instant coffee powder
1 tbsp sugar
4 tbsp warm water

For the cream cheese
½ litre full fat milk
½ tsp citric acid crystals

For the garnish
1 tsp cocoa powder

For the cream cheese
1. Put the milk to boil in a thick-bottomed pan.
2. When it comes to a boil, remove from the flame and keep aside for a few minutes.
3. In another bowl, dissolve the citric acid crystals in ¼ cup of warm water.
4. Pour this mixture into the hot milk and allow to stand for about 5 minutes till the milk curdles on its own. Stir gently if required.
5. Strain this mixture using a muslin cloth. Do not squeeze out all the water.
6. Blend the hot drained milk solids in a food processor till smooth and creamy. Keep aside.

How to proceed
1. Cut a thin round of the sponge cake. Keep aside.
2. Cut the remaining sponge cake into 12 mm. X 50 mm. (½" x 2") long fingers.
3. Arrange the cake fingers on a baking tray and toast in a pre-heated oven at 160°C (320°F) for 20 minutes or till crisp. Allow them to cool.
4. In a pan, heat the Marsala wine with 5 tbsp sugar over gentle heat until the sugar has dissolved. Allow to cool.
5. Whip the cream until soft peaks form. Keep refrigerated.

6. Whisk the cream cheese and wine mixture together. Gently fold in the whipped cream. Keep aside.
7. Arrange the cake round on the base of a 200 mm. (8") diameter serving dish. Soak generously with the coffee soaking syrup.
8. Top with half of the cream cheese-wine mixture. Freeze for 30 minutes until it has set.
9. Dip each piece of toasted cake finger in the coffee soaking syrup for 10 seconds.
10. Arrange the soaked cake fingers over the first layer of cream cheese. Top with the remaining cream cheese-wine mixture. Freeze for 4 to 6 hours until set.
11. Sprinkle the cocoa powder on top. Cut into squares and serve immediately.

MENU 5

No Fuss American

Two in a Bowl Soup

Crunchy Salad

Pasta and Vegetable Casserole

Celery Garlic Toasts

Cream and Brownie in a Glass

TWO IN A BOWL SOUP : Recipe on page 67. →

About the Menu....

America really doesn't have a cuisine of its own, having adopted food cultures from around the world and modified them to suit the fast paced lifestyle of its population. This simple no-fuss menu is a combination of quick and healthy American favourites.

Clever presentation is key to the Two in a Bowl Soup where two thick soups are served side by side in the same bowl without getting mixed! The Crunchy Salad uses nutritious vegetables like spinach, iceberg lettuce and tomatoes, while the baked Pasta and Vegetable Casserole introduces some more wholesome vegetables into the meal. Celery Garlic Toast makes a great accompaniment to the soup, and in an informal setting, can be dunked into it without any guilt! Brownies are the most popular all-American dessert and acquire surprising sophistication when served in a parfait glass with lashings of fresh cream.

An informal gathering of friends is ideally suited to an American theme. Add a denim dress code, some popular music, and chip and dip, and you have an easygoing party underway.

Two in a Bowl Soup

Picture on page 65.

Preparation time: 20 minutes. Cooking time: 30 minutes. Serves 4.

For the potato soup
1 cup peeled and cubed potatoes
1 tsp chopped garlic
1 cup chopped onions
½ tsp dry red chilli flakes
1½ cups milk
2 tbsp oil
Salt to taste

For the broccoli soup
2 cups broccoli florets
½ onion, chopped
1 tbsp plain flour (maida)
2 tbsp butter
Salt and pepper to taste

For the potato soup
1. Heat the oil in a pan, add the garlic and onions and sauté for a few minutes.
2. Add the potatoes and sauté for a few more minutes.
3. Add 1½ cups of water and salt and simmer till the potatoes are cooked.
4. Cool the potato mixture and blend to a smooth purée in a mixer with the milk.
5. Add the chilli flakes and keep aside.

For the broccoli soup

1. Heat the butter in a pan, add the onion and sauté for a few minutes.
2. Add the broccoli and stir for 4 to 5 minutes.
3. Sprinkle the flour over the broccoli and continue stirring for another 2 minutes.
4. Add 2 cups of water, stirring continuously.
5. Simmer till the broccoli is tender and add the salt and pepper.
6. Cool slightly and blend to a smooth purée in a mixer.
   Keep aside.

How to proceed

1. Re-heat both the soups separately.
2. Carefully pour both the soups on opposite sides of the bowl, so that both the soups have a line of differentiation.
3. Repeat with three other bowls.
   Serve hot.

Handy tip : Both the soups should be thick so that they do not mix easily.

Crunchy Salad

Preparation time: 5 minutes. No cooking. Serves 4.

½ cup shredded spinach (*palak*) or arugula lettuce
2 cups torn iceberg or any other lettuce
1 cup bean sprouts, cleaned
4 cherry tomatoes
2 tbsp pumpkin seeds
4 pretzels or bread sticks, broken into pieces

To be mixed into a honey-lemon dressing
1 tbsp honey
2 tbsp lemon juice
2 tbsp chopped spring onion greens
1 tsp salt

1. Mix the spinach, iceberg and bean sprouts in a bowl.
2. Put some ice water in the bowl and keep in the refrigerator.
3. Just before serving, drain the spinach, iceberg and bean sprouts.

4. Add the cherry tomatoes, pumpkin seeds and pretzel sticks an place in a serving bowl.
5. Pour the dressing on top.

Handy tip : To make this salad more nutritious, you can add *paneer* (cottage cheese) cubes to it.

Pasta and Vegetable Casserole

Preparation time: 15 minutes. Cooking time: 30 minutes. Serves 4.
Baking temperature : 200°C (400°F). Baking time : 25 to 30 minutes.

2 cups cooked pasta (penne, fusilli etc.)

For the roasted vegetables
2 cups blanched, peeled and quartered tomatoes
½ cup red capsicum cubes
½ cup green capsicum cubes
½ cup onion cubes
2 tbsp chopped garlic
3 tsp olive oil
1 tsp sugar
Salt to taste

For baking
4 tbsp grated cheese

For the cheese sauce
1 tbsp plain flour *(maida)*
2 cups milk
4 tbsp grated cheese
2 tbsp butter
Salt and freshly ground pepper to taste

For the roasted vegetables

1. Combined all the ingredients in a baking tray and toss well.
2. Bake in a pre-heated oven at 200°C (400°F) for 10 to 15 minutes, stirring once in between.

For the cheese sauce

1. Melt the butter in a pan, add the flour and sauté on a slow flame for ½ minute or till you get the aroma of cooked flour.
2. Add the milk gradually, while stirring continuously, so that lumps do not form. Bring to a boil.
3. Add the cheese, salt and pepper, mix well and heat till the sauce thickens. Keep aside.

How to proceed

1. Spread a layer of the roasted vegetables in a baking dish.
2. Top with the cooked pasta.
3. Cover with the cheese sauce and top with the grated cheese. Bake in a pre-heated oven at 200°C (400°F) for 10 minutes.
   Serve hot.

Celery Garlic Toasts

Preparation time: 5 minutes. Cooking time: 15 minutes. Makes 16.
Baking temperature : 180°C (360°F). Baking time : 15 minutes.

8 slices of whole wheat bread

To be coarsely ground into a paste
½ cup chopped celery
2 to 3 cloves garlic
¼ cup softened butter
Salt to taste

1. Apply the ground celery-garlic paste equally on all the toasts.
2. Bake in a pre-heated oven at 180°C (360°F) for 10 minutes or till the toasts are evenly browned.
   Cut into halves and serve immediately.

Cream and Brownie in a Glass

Preparation time: 25 minutes. Cooking time: 35 minutes. Makes 8.
Baking temperature : 180°C (360°F). Baking time : 25 to 30 minutes.

For the chocolate brownie
1 cup plain flour (*maida*)
¼ cup cocoa powder
¾ cup powdered sugar
½ tsp soda bi-carb
½ tsp baking powder
6 tbsp fresh thick curds (*dahi*)
5 tbsp milk
5 tbsp melted butter
½ cup chopped walnuts (*akhrot*)
½ tsp vanilla essence

Other ingredients
2 cups fresh cream, chilled
4 tbsp powdered sugar
¼ tsp vanilla essence
8 canned peach halves

For the garnish
4 cocktail cherries

SOM TOM (Green Papaya Salad) : Recipe on page 95. →

For the chocolate brownie

1. Mix all the ingredients in a mixing bowl using a wooden spoon. Make sure there are no lumps.
2. Pour this mixture into the greased and dusted 200 mm. x 200 mm. (8″ x 8″) baking tray.
3. Bake it in a pre-heated oven for 20 to 25 minutes.
4. Cool and cut into 20 mm. x 20 mm. (¾″ x ¾″) pieces. Keep aside.

How to proceed

1. Whip the cream in a bowl till it doubles in volume and forms soft peaks.
2. Carefully add the sugar and vanilla essence.
3. Fill into a piping bag and keep aside.
4. Pipe out some cream into each tall glass.
5. Place a few brownie squares and top with a peach half.
6. Repeat steps 4 and 5.
7. Garnish with a cocktail cherry and serve chilled.

Handy tip : If you are in a hurry, use a ready-made brownie.

MENU 6

Arabian Delights

About the Menu....

Middle Eastern cuisine combines the sophistication and subtleties of European cuisine with the exotic ingredients of the Middle and Far East. The result is fresh, flavourful and infinitely diverse.

This elegant menu combines the cuisine of different Middle Eastern countries, beginning with Hummus, the popular chickpea dip that can be served with the our version of Lavash or any other thin crisp bread. Labneh is another well-liked dip made from hung curds, garlic and sesame seeds that complements crisp fried vegetables. Tabbouleh is a commonly found broken wheat salad that develops a whole new appeal here with the addition of tangy oranges. Falafel, spiced chickpea patties stuffed in warm soft pita bread pockets, makes a satisfying main course. Dessert is the phenomenally rich but delectable Baklava, a highly sweetened combination of filo pastry and nuts. For those who find filo pastry difficult to acquire or make, we've introduced a mock version using ready-to-use samosa patties.

An Arabian night would mean dim lights, low seating, gauzy drapes, incense, and hookahs. If well orchestrated it can be a truly memorable experience.

Herbed Hummus with Sesame Lavash

Preparation time: 20 minutes. Cooking time: 20 minutes. Serves 4.
Baking temperature : 180°C (360°F). Baking time: 15 minutes.

For the herbed humus
¼ cup *kabuli chana* (chick peas*)*
Juice of ½ lemon
2 tbsp fresh thick curds *(dahi)*
1 clove garlic
½ cup finely chopped parsley
1 tsp oregano
Salt to taste

For the garnish
A pinch of chilli powder
1 tbsp olive oil

For the sesame lavash
¼ cup whole wheat flour (*gehun ka atta*)
1 tsp black sesame (*til*) seeds
1 tsp oil
Salt to taste

Other ingredients
whole wheat flour (gehun ka atta)
for rolling

For the herbed humus

1. Soak the *kabuli chana* in water for 6 hours.
2. Drain and cook the in a pressure cooker with a little salt. Cool and drain.

Keep the strained liquid aside.

3. Combine the lemon juice, curds, garlic, parsley, oregano, cooked *kabuli chana,* oil, salt and some of the strained liquid in a mixer and blend until smooth. If the mixture is too thick, add 1 to 2 tbsp more of the strained liquid.
4. Garnished with the chilli powder and olive oil. Keep aside.

For the sesame lavash

1. Combine the whole wheat flour, oil and salt and just enough water to knead into a firm dough.
2. Divide the dough into 4 equal potions and roll out each potion into very thin rounds with help of a little whole wheat flour.
3. Sprinkle sesame seeds on each round and cut each into 6 wedges like one would cut a pizza.
4. Bake them in a pre-heated oven on a lightly greased baking tray at 180°C (360°F) for 10 to 12 minutes or till they are crisp and lightly browned.
5. Repeat for the remaining portions to make all the lavash.
6. Cool and store in an air tight container.

   Serve with herbed humus.

Labneh with Crispy Vegetables

Picture on page 85.

Preparation time: 20 minutes. Cooking time: 5 minutes. Serves 4.

For the labneh
½ cup thick hung curds *(chakka)*
2 tsp fresh cream
2 cloves garlic, grated
1 tsp roasted sesame (*til*) seeds
1 tbsp olive oil
Salt to taste

For the crispy vegetables
1 cup thinly sliced rounds of mixed vegetables (carrots, baby corn, zucchini, small brinjals, yellow squash)
½ cup corn flour
Salt to taste

Other ingredients
Oil for deep-frying

For the labneh

1. Pound the sesame seeds and olive oil in a mortar and pestle to a paste.
2. Add all the remaining ingredients and whisk well.
3. Refrigerate to chill.

For the crispy vegetables

1. Heat the oil in a wok or a *kadai*.
2. Spread ¼ cup of sliced vegetables on a flat plate.
3. Sprinkle some cornflour and salt over it and mix well.
4. Deep-fry in hot oil till crisp and golden brown.
5. Repeat for all the vegetables. Drain on absorbent paper and serve immediately with the chilled labneh.

Orange Sesame Tabouleh

Preparation time: 15 minutes. No cooking. Makes 1 cup.

1 cup broken wheat *(dalia)*
1 tbsp grated orange zest
2 tbsp toasted sesame *(til)* seeds
½ cup chopped spring onions
¼ cup tomato cubes
½ cup finely chopped parsley
2 tbsp lemon juice
2 tbsp olive oil
2 tbsp orange squash
Salt to taste

1. Cook the broken wheat in 1½ cups of water for 10 minutes till it is tender.
2. Drain and pour cold water over to cool it. Drain again and keep aside.
3. Combine all the ingredients in a bowl and mix well.

4. Refrigerate for at least 1 hour before serving so that all the flavours blend.

Handy tips : 1. While grating the orange zest, be careful not to grate the while pith, as it is bitter.
2. If cous-cous is available, use that instead of broken wheat *(dalia)*.

LABNEH WITH CRISPY VEGETABLES : Recipe on page 81. →

Falafel

Preparation time: 25 minutes. Cooking time: 30 minutes. Serves 4.

For the pita bread
1 cup whole wheat flour *(gehun ka atta)*
1 tsp crumbled (5 grams) fresh yeast
½ tsp sugar
1 tbsp oil
½ tsp salt

For the dressing
6 tbsp fresh thick curds *(dahi)*
2 cloves garlic, chopped
¼ cup chopped spring onions (including greens)
A pinch of sugar
Salt to taste

For the patties
1 cup *kabuli chana* (chick peas), soaked overnight and drained
½ tsp chopped green chillies
½ cup chopped mint leaves (phudina)
½ tsp grated garlic
½ cup grated cabbage
1 cup grated carrot
¼ cup finely chopped capsicum
½ tsp roasted cumin seed *(jeera)* powder
salt to taste

Other ingredients
Oil for deep-frying
½ cup thinly sliced tomatoes
1 cup shredded lettuce

For the pita bread

1. Combine all the ingredients except the oil in a bowl and using enough water, knead into a soft dough until it is smooth and elastic (approx. 5 to 7 minutes).
2. Add the oil and knead again.
3. Cover the dough with a wet muslin cloth and allow it to prove till it doubles in volume (approx. 15 to 20 minutes).
4. Press the dough lightly to remove air and divide into 6 equal parts.
5. Roll out each portion into circle of 150 mm. (6″) in diameter and 4 mm. (1/6″) thickness.
6. Cook on a hot *tava* (griddle) on each side for a minute or until the bread puffs up.
7. Remove and keep aside.
8. Cut each pita bread into 2 halves and keep aside.

For the dressing

Blend all the ingredients in a mixer to get a smooth sauce. Keep refrigerated

For the patties

1. Combine the *kabuli chana,* green chillies and mint and blend in mixer to a coarse past without using water.
2. Add the remaining ingredients and mix well.
3. Divide the mixture into 12 equal parts and shape them into patties.

4. Deep-fry the patties in hot oil till golden brown in colour.
5. Drain on absorbent paper and keep aside.

How to proceed

1. Warm the pita bread halves on a hot (*tava*) griddle.
2. Fill each pita bread half with some tomato slices and shredded lettuce, one patty and a spoonful of the dressing on top.
3. Repeat for the remaining pita bread halves and other ingredients to make 11 more falafels.

   Serve immediately.

Baklava

Preparation time: 25 minutes. Cooking time: 20 minutes. Serves 4.

4 ready-made frozen samosa pattis
2 tbsp cornflour dissolved in 1 tbsp water

For the filling
¼ cup chopped walnuts (*akhrot*)
¼ cup soaked and chopped figs (*anjeer*)
¼ cup soaked and chopped apricots
¼ cup chopped dates
A pinch cinnamon *(dalchini)* powder
2 tbsp honey
2 tbsp brown sugar
1 tsp lemon juice

Other ingredients
Oil for deep-frying
Honey for drizzling

1. Make a thick paste of corn flour and water. Keep aside.
2. Cut each samosa patti into 3 to get 75 mm. x 62 mm. (3″ x 2½″) rectangles.
3. Mix all the ingredients for the filling together and divide into 6 equal portions.
4. Place the filling on one rectangle taking care to leave the sides clean.
5. Place another piece of samosa patti on top and seal the edges using the corn flour mixture.
6. Repeat with other rectangles to make 5 more baklavas.
7. Deep-fry the baklavas in hot oil until golden colour. Drain on absorbent paper Drizzle with honey and serve hot.

MENU 7

Try Thai

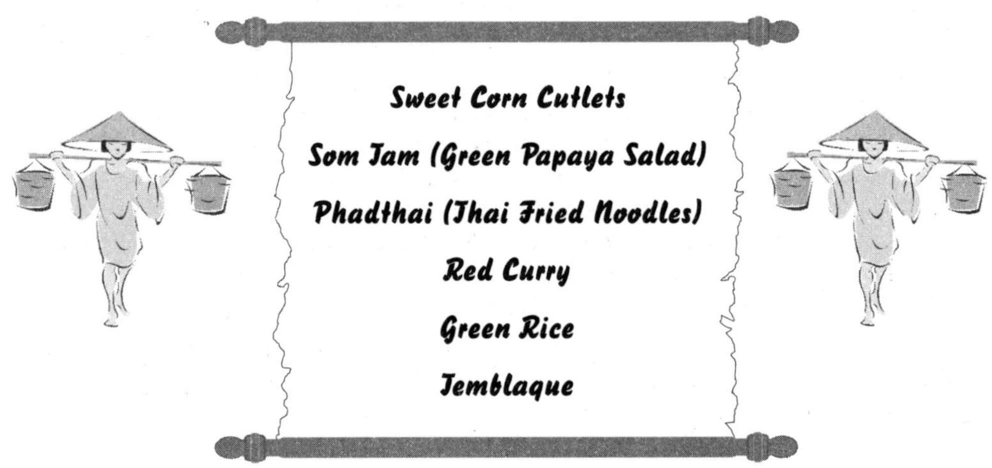

Sweet Corn Cutlets

Som Tam (Green Papaya Salad)

Phadthai (Thai Fried Noodles)

Red Curry

Green Rice

Temblaque

About the Menu....

Delicate and superbly colourful, Thai food has been influenced by Chinese, Malay and Indian cuisine. The Thais believe that food must please the eye as well as the taste buds and take great care to prepare and present their dishes attractively.

This easy-to-cook menu starts with shallow fried Sweet Corn Cutlets that must be served immediately. A favourite at Thai restaurants, the Green Papaya Salad is an interesting combination of unripe papaya tossed in soya sauce and tamarind flavoured dressing. Thai Fried Noodles are soft noodles combined with bean curd and crunchy peanuts that give it a distinctly different taste from noodles cooked in other Oriental styles. Adding colour to the meal is the spicy Red Curry that perfectly complements the subtle flavour of Green Rice. The meal ends with a coconut-based dessert called Temblaque that must be served with a fruit purée.

An important aspect of a Thai meal is a beautifully carved fruit and vegetable centrepiece try your hand at it or source it from an expert. Other touches could include coconut place settings and mats and plentiful flowers the more exotic the better!

Sweet Corn Cutlets

Preparation time: 5 minutes.   Cooking time: 30 minutes.   Serves 4.

For the cutlets
¾ cup cream style sweet corn
3 tbsp cornflour
Salt to taste

For the tempura batter
2 tbsp plain flour *(maida)*
¼ cup cornflour
Salt to taste

Other ingredients
Oil for greasing and deep-frying

For the cutlets

1. Mix together the cream style sweet corn, cornflour and salt and blend in a mixer to a coarse paste.

2. Pour into a greased 150 mm. x 150 mm. (6″ x 6″) square thali and steam for 10 minutes in a steamer.
3. Remove from the steamer, cool and cut into 25 mm. x 25 mm. (1″ x 1″) square pieces.

For the tempura batter

Mix the ingredients with enough water to get a batter of coating consistency.

How to proceed

1. Dip the cutlets in the tempura batter and deep-fry in hot oil till golden brown.
2. Drain on absorbent paper.

   Serve hot with a sauce of your choice.

Som Tam (Green Papaya Salad)

Picture on page 75.

Preparation time: 15 to 20 minutes. No cooking. Serves 4 to 6.

3 cups peeled and grated raw papaya
¼ cup thinly sliced tomatoes
½ cup sliced long beans (*chawli*)
½ tbsp finely chopped green chillies
½ cup crushed roasted peanuts
2 tbsp sugar
1 tbsp tamarind (*imli*) pulp
1 tsp chilli powder
1 tbsp soya sauce
2 tbsp lemon juice
2 tbsp chopped coriander
Salt to taste

1. Combine the ingredients and toss well.
2. Store refrigerated till use.
   Serve chilled.

Phadthai (Thai Fried Noodles)

Preparation time: 10 minutes. Cooking time: 10 minutes. Serves 4.

3 cups cooked rice noodles, *refer handy tip*
1 cup tofu (soya *paneer)* cubes
2 crushed garlic cloves
4 spring onions, chopped
1 cup bean sprouts
2 tbsp roasted peanuts, chopped
¾ tsp chilli powder
2 tsp sugar
2 tbsp soya sauce
1 tbsp lemon juice
4 tbsp oil
Salt to taste

Other ingredients
Oil for deep-frying

For the garnish
2 tbsp chopped coriander
2 tbsp roasted peanuts, chopped
1 lemon wedge

1. Fry the tofu cubes in hot oil for a couple of minutes. Drain on absorbent paper and keep aside.
2. Heat the oil in a wok on a high flame and add the crushed garlic.
3. Add the fried tofu, spring onions, beans sprouts, peanuts and noodles.
4. Add the chilli powder, sugar, soya sauce, lemon juice and salt and toss well. Serve hot garnished with coriander, peanuts and the lemon wedge.

Handy tip: To cook rice noodles, soak them in boiling hot water for 10 to 15 minutes or as the instruction on the package specify. Drain the water and again dip into cold water in order to arrest any further cooking.
Drain and use as required.

Red Curry

Preparation time: 20 minutes. Cooking time: 15 minutes. Serves 6.

6 to 7 tbsp red curry paste, given below
2 cups coconut milk
1 tbsp cornflour
½ tsp soya sauce
½ cup chopped basil leaves
½ cup baby corn cubes
½ cup brinjal (*baingan*) cubes
1 cup broccoli florets
½ cup sliced mushrooms
1 tbsp oil
Salt to taste

For the red curry paste
5 red chillies, soaked in warm water for 10 minutes and drained
¼ cup chopped onions
2 peeled garlic cloves
½ tbsp grated ginger

1 stalk lemon grass
3 stalks coriander
1 tbsp coriander (*dhania*) seeds
2 tbsp cumin (*jeera*) seeds
½ tbsp white pepper
½ tsp salt

For the red curry paste

Grind all the ingredients to a paste with a mortar and pestle or in a mixer using a little water. Keep aside.

How to proceed

1. Dissolve the cornflour in the coconut milk. Keep aside.
2. Heat the oil in a large pan, add the red curry paste and fry for a few minutes.
3. Add the cornflour-coconut milk mixture, soya sauce, basil leaves and all the vegetables.
4. Simmer for 10 minutes till the vegetables are tender.
5. Add salt and boil for 2 minutes till the curry thickens.
   Serve hot.

Green Rice

Preparation time: 10 minutes. Cooking time: 15 minutes. Serves 4.

1½ cups Basmati rice, soaked for 1 hour
3 cups coconut milk
1 bayleaf *(tejpatta)*
4 tbsp chopped coriander
4 tbsp chopped mint (*phudina*) leaves
½ tbsp finely chopped green chillies
2 tbsp oil
1 tsp salt

For the garnish
Lemon wedges

1. Wash and drain the rice.
2. Heat the oil in a pan, add the rice and fry for 4 to 5 minutes.
3. Add the coconut milk, bay leaf and salt and cook on a show flame with the lid on till all the liquid is absorbed.
4. Lower the heat as much as possible, cover the pan and cook for 10 more minutes. Remove the bayleaf and discard it.
5. Add in the coriander, mint and green chillies and mix well.
   Serve hot garnished with lemon wedges.

Temblaque

Preparation time: 10 minutes. Cooking time: 5 minutes. Serves 4 to 6
Setting time: 120 minutes.

3 cups coconut milk
½ cup sugar
½ cup cornflour

For the mango sauce (for serving)
2 medium sized mangoes, puréed and strained
2 tbsp dark rum

For the strawberry sauce (for serving)
1½ cups strawberries, puréed and strained
½ cup sugar
2 tbsp dark rum (optional)

For the mango sauce (for serving)
Flavour the mango purée with rum and refrigerate overnight.

For the strawberry sauce (for serving)
Add the sugar to the strawberry purée with rum mix well and refrigerate overnight.

How to proceed

1. Mix all the ingredients in a non-stick pan and heat, stirring constantly on a low flame.
2. Stir till the mixture is thick enough to coat the back of a spoon.
3. Cool and pour the custard into individual moulds.
4. Refrigerate for 2 hours or until set.
5. Unmould and serve with both the sauces.

Mini Series by *Tarla Dalal*

Healthy Breakfast

Healthy Snacks

Healthy
Soups & Salads

Healthy Juices

Fast Foods
Made Healthy

Calcium
Rich Recipes

Iron Rich Recipes

Forever Young Diet

Home Remedies

Low Cholesterol
Recipes